TOP YOUTUBE STARS™

JENNA MARBLES

Comedian with More than
3 BILLION VIEWS

ADAM FURGANG

rosen publishing's
rosen central®

New York

Published in 2020 by The Rosen Publishing Group, Inc.
29 East 21st Street, New York, NY 10010

Copyright © 2020 by The Rosen Publishing Group, Inc.

First Edition

Library of Congress Cataloging-in-Publication Data

Names: Furgang, Adam, author.
Title: Jenna Marbles: Comedian with More than 3 Billion Views / Adam Furgang.
Description: First edition. | New York : Rosen Central, 2020. | Series: Top YouTube stars | Includes bibliographical references and index.
Identifiers: LCCN 2018051628| ISBN 9781725346253 (library bound) | ISBN 9781725346246 (pbk.)
Subjects: LCSH: Marbles, Jenna, 1986– —Juvenile literature. | Comedians—United States—Biography—Juvenile literature. | Internet personalities—United States—Biography—Juvenile literature. | YouTube (Electronic resource)—Biography—Juvenile literature.
Classification: LCC PN2287.M46 F87 2019 | DDC 791.092 [B]—dc23
LC record available at https://lccn.loc.gov/2018051628

Manufactured in the United States of America

On the cover: YouTube comedian Jenna Marbles (whose hair is sometimes pink and sometimes other colors) pauses for a photo while attending the 2015 Streamy Awards in Los Angeles, California.

CONTENTS

Have you ever seen the YouTube videos "A Full Face of Rhinestones" or "Making Terrible Hot Glue Crafts"? What about "Following a Bob Ross Painting Tutorial" or "Just Trying to Blend in with My Green Screen"? These videos, and hundreds more, are just some of the silly and playful videos created by Jenna Marbles—one of the most famous YouTube stars in the world. These videos can all be found on her YouTube channel, which she updates regularly.

Marbles is best known for her whimsical commentary, how-to makeup videos, and unique style of comedy skits and parodies. Marbles also posts videos about her own life, in which she often reveals many personal details about her childhood, family, intimate thoughts, and musings regarding her journey to become a YouTube star.

Marbles, whose real last name is Mourey, first started using YouTube as a platform to share her homemade videos in 2010. At that point, YouTube was still a fairly new online service. As of March 2019, Marbles's YouTube channel had more than nineteen million subscribers, and her videos have been collectively viewed more than three billion times.

Marbles also hosts her own talk show on SiriusXM satellite radio and has appeared in person at numerous conventions and awards shows. She also maintains social media accounts on Instagram, Facebook, and Twitter, all of which have millions of followers. It was estimated in 2018 that Marbles had a net worth of over $2.9 million. Her earnings come from the YouTube partner program, which runs advertising before her videos.

The online video-sharing service YouTube first began back in 2004 when PayPal employees Jawed Karim, Steve Chen, and Chad Hurley wanted to share videos in a single location on the internet. At the time, no website existed

In addition to her YouTube channel, Jenna Marbles also hosts a weekly SiriusXM pop-music radio show, *YouTube 15*. Marbles is seen here visiting the radio station in 2014 when her show first debuted.

for easily sharing videos, so Karim, Chen, and Hurley set out to create it. In 2005, the trio launched YouTube. The website was an instant success, and within one year Google announced it was buying YouTube for $1.6 billion worth of stock. Fast-forward to 2018, and YouTube has grown to become one of the most popular destinations on the internet. According to YouTube, the video-sharing service has "over a billion users—almost one-third of all people on the Internet—and each day those users watch a billion hours of video, generating billions of views."

In the past, radio, television, and the movies served as the mediums for people to become famous. Today, ordinary citizens have made themselves famous just by performing, talking, and even playing video games on YouTube. This new media outlet is also a new form of entertainment and has become extremely popular among younger people. According to YouTube, "18–34 year olds are watching YouTube on mobile [devices] and it reaches more people in the US than any TV network."

Jenna Marbles, and many other YouTube stars like her, are part of a new wave of homegrown DIY (do-it-yourself) entertainers who are changing what we watch and how we watch it.

CHAPTER ONE

A Brief History of Jenna Marbles

One of the keys to Jenna Marbles's success as a YouTube star has been her willingness to disclose her private life to her audience. Marbles's fans—mostly teenage and young adult girls—often describe her as genuine. In some of Marbles's videos, she answers fans' questions, as well as disclosing personal details about her family, life, and childhood. One of Marbles's popular autobiographical videos was published on her YouTube channel on March 28, 2013, and is called "Draw My Life—Jenna Marbles." As of September 2018, the video had been viewed over fifteen million times.

MARBLES'S ORIGIN

Marbles's parents are Thomas and Deborah Mourey. The two met, married, and settled in Rochester, New York, where they started a family. First they had a son, Devin, in 1984. Two years later, on September 15, 1986, Jenna Nicole Mourey was born.

Growing up, Marbles's father worked for the photography company Eastman Kodak as a chemist. In her YouTube video

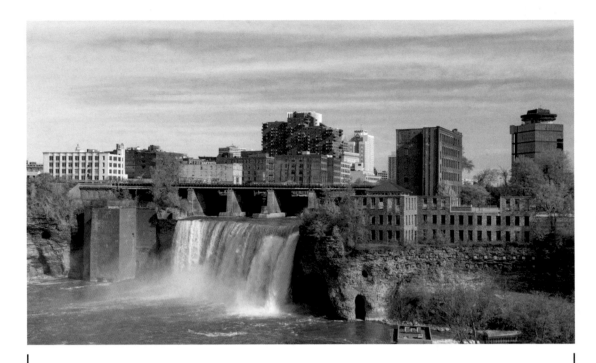

Jenna Marbles's hometown, Rochester, New York, is located on the southern shore of Lake Ontario. Part of the scenic Finger Lakes region, it is the state's third-largest city.

"Draw My Life—Jenna Marbles," Marbles said, "My dad loves Subarus and he's also a chemist, and he has lots of really cool patents for things like polymers that I don't really understand."

When Marbles was still young, her parents divorced, and her mother raised her and her brother. Marbles's father remarried, and her mother has had a steady boyfriend for a very long time. Marbles mentions her parents' divorce in her video, saying that it "worked out alright" and "everyone wound up pretty happy."

While Marbles was growing up, her mother, Deborah, worked in various jobs, including teaching strategic digital marketing to undergraduate and graduate students. Deborah Mourey also runs her own strategic marketing consulting company.

MARBLES'S CHILDHOOD RECOLLECTIONS

Sharing personal stories, even uncomfortable or embarrassing ones, is one of the reasons Marbles's YouTube videos are so popular. While growing up, Marbles enjoyed many creative and theater arts–based hobbies. She was involved with gymnastics, dancing, and playing musical instruments such as the piano and the clarinet. She also loved animals and hoped to work with them as a zookeeper or a veterinarian when she got older. Every year for her birthday, she would make a wish after blowing out her birthday cake candles, hoping she could one day get a dog or a cat. Due to her mother's allergies to animals, she could not get one while growing up. Her father eventually got a cat, but Marbles described it as not very friendly,

Jenna Marbles took her last name from her dog, Mr. Marbles. Here Marbles is pictured with her other famous dog, a Chihuahua named Kermit.

sometimes scratching her brother and her on the face. As an adult, Marbles would eventually have several dogs.

Growing up, Marbles also enjoyed sports. She liked playing baseball, and her father coached the team she was on.

"MEET MY MOM"

In a Thanksgiving video on Marbles's YouTube page from November 26, 2014, titled "The Mom Tag—Meet My Mom," Marbles's mother, Deborah Mourey, appears as a guest alongside Marbles and answers some questions asked by fans. During the video, Marbles and her mom reveal their close relationship while playfully poking one another and candidly revealing funny family stories, such as the following:

- If Jenna had been born a boy, her name was going to be Benjamin.
- A squirrel once climbed down the chimney, and Marbles caught it in a pillowcase.
- Her family has a history of being thrifty and reusing old birthday cards that were originally given to other people. According to Deborah Mourey, "Well, my grandmother used to cut out the name … and then my mother … took it a step further, and she would just photocopy the card, and then give you that."

GRADE SCHOOL MARBLES

In the YouTube video "Draw My Life—Jenna Marbles," Marbles drew on a whiteboard while she described her grade school and high school years.

One year, Marbles broke her nose while attempting to perform a back flip off a dock at her father's lake house. During the back flip, Marbles hit her face on a ladder and, as a result, has a small T-shaped scar above her nose.

Marbles's best friend was named Brittany, and they played volleyball and softball together. While talking about her best friend from grade school in her YouTube video, Marbles drew a stick figure on the whiteboard of herself and Brittany as "two peas in a pod."

Marbles went on to describe how she felt out of place in school because she was not in the advanced classes. According to Marbles, "I took regular classes, and sort of felt like I didn't fit in."

In her video, Marbles described liking a boy who did not like her back. She would often wait outside his locker before homeroom. According to Marbles, "In one quarter where there are sixty days, I had fifty-two tardies because I was just waiting for him at his locker."

After grade school, Marbles attended Brighton High School in Rochester, New York. During high school, her best friend dropped out, and Marbles was left feeling lonely. In the ninth grade, Marbles met a boy named Willie in her gym class. The two began dating, and the relationship lasted throughout Marbles's four years in high school. The couple broke up when high school ended, and they each moved away to go to different colleges. After graduating high school in 2004, Marbles wanted to go to college in a new city. Her next step in life at age seventeen would take her off to Boston, Massachusetts.

CHAPTER TWO

Mourey Transforms into Marbles

A fter graduating from high school, Marbles moved to Boston to attend college at Suffolk University. Marbles was only seventeen years old when she went away, and she didn't know anyone at the school. She soon made friends after becoming involved with a sport she loved—softball. A spark of what would be in Marbles's future started when she purchased herself an Apple MacBook laptop. Using the computer, she soon began to teach herself how to edit short videos using the Apple video editing software iMovie. This was the beginning of what would eventually become a lucrative career for Marbles. At Suffolk University, Marbles earned an undergraduate degree in psychology and graduated in 2008.

Marbles continued with her education and attended Boston University, where she earned a master's degree in sports psychology and counseling. After graduating in 2010, she decided she wanted to continue living in Boston. Finding work in her field of sports psychology was not easy, so she took various jobs to help earn enough money to live. For a while, Marbles was struggling to pay her bills.

After shooting video footage and then working on an Apple MacBook, Jenna Marbles trained herself to edit short videos. Eventually, Marbles would use her skills to start her own YouTube channel.

According to an article by Amy O'Leary in the *New York Times:*

In the summer of 2010, Ms. Mourey [Marbles] shared a three-bedroom apartment in Cambridge, Massachusetts, where her $800 rent was scrounged together from a patchwork of part-time gigs: bartending, blogging, go-go dancing at nightclubs and working at a tanning salon, where she remembers the singularly depressing chore of mopping up customers' sweat. Meanwhile, her newly completed master's degree in sports psychology gathered dust.

Jenna Marbles has always enjoyed sports. Her first job out of school was working for Barstool Sports, where she started blogging and learned about comedy from her boss, Dave Portnoy.

Marbles had been applying for better jobs, and good news eventually came when Dave Portnoy called her and offered her a job at Barstool Sports. Portnoy, who is also known on his website as El Presidente, is the founder of Barstool Sports, a satirical website that concentrates on sports news and entertainment. Marbles began working as Portnoy's assistant and learned a lot during her time there. Portnoy helped teach Marbles many things about the internet and writing blogs, as well as how to be funny in online blogs and videos. Marbles disclosed in her "Draw My Life" video that she was so happy when she got the job that she cried.

At Barstool Sports, Marbles wrote blogs and started to produce videos for the website. Some of Marbles's videos created at Barstool Sports can still be found online by

"CHARLES FRANKLIN MARBLES IS A SAD SAD MAN"

Everything Marbles learned while working at Barstool Sports helped her in her future career making videos for YouTube. Marbles uploaded her very first video on her personal YouTube page on February 17, 2010. The video, titled "Charles Franklin Marbles Is a Sad Sad Man," is of her dog, Mr. Marbles, finding and then losing a stuffed animal named Mr. Lion. The satirical video is similar to silent films, with no dialogue, and simple text narration intercut throughout footage of Marbles's dog and a stuffed lion. The only audio is the Henry Mancini song "Love Theme from Romeo and Juliet," which plays continually throughout the video. The two-and-a-half-minute video ends with the word "Fin," which means "End" in French. She had not started using the last name Marbles for herself yet, and the video ends with a single credit, "By Jenna Mourey."

When she was younger, Jenna Marbles could not have a dog. When she got older, she got a Chihuahua, which has since been in many of her YouTube videos.

searching for them though Google. In one YouTube video called "Barstool Sports Street Interviews" from May 4, 2010, Marbles conducted street interviews outside a Boston Bruins hockey game.

Marbles continued to make her own videos. One day while heading home after work, Marbles had an idea for a video that would go on to change her life.

A NEW LAST NAME

So, what made Jenna Mourey start posting videos under the name Jenna Marbles? While looking for a new job, her mother, Deborah Mourey, voiced concerns about privacy and explained how her daughter's videos were coming up when she typed her own name on Google. She worried any association with the videos could hinder her employment prospects. Jenna Mourey agreed with her mom and began using the pseudonym Jenna Marbles for her YouTube channel.

The name Marbles comes from her dog, a Chihuahua named Mr. Marbles. Mr. Marbles the Chihuahua was actually named after a ventriloquist dummy named Mr. Marbles in an episode of the TV show *Seinfeld* titled "The Chicken Roaster."

"HOW TO TRICK PEOPLE INTO THINKING YOU'RE GOOD LOOKING"

On July 9, 2010, Marbles uploaded the video "How to Trick People into Thinking You're Good Looking." The satirical video is not intended to be taken seriously.

The video begins with Marbles saying, "If you were born really ugly like me, have no fear. There's steps you can take to be good-looking. Kind of."

While Marbles's video commentary is often self-deprecating, with her continually saying she—and the audience—are "ugly," Marbles maintains a comical tone throughout the video.

During the two-and-a-half minute video (which is filled with profanity), Marbles undergoes a facial transformation after applying heavy makeup and blow-drying her hair straight. Marbles's commentary throughout the video is funny and sarcastic, and it pokes fun at the expectations society places on women's looks. Marbles never actually demonstrates how to apply makeup or blow-dry her hair in the video, and all of the transitions are accomplished with simple jump cuts.

Marbles continues to explain how she has already bleached her hair blond and tanned her skin so she would not "look like an albino." Marbles then puts on and removes her eyeglasses while explaining a switch to contact lenses. Marbles then says, "Step one. Take a shower. Because you're probably dirty." Afterward, she transitions from not wearing makeup on her face with quick jump cuts to suddenly having heavy makeup, dark black eye shadow, eyeliner, fake eyelashes, and finally, lipstick. Marbles's hair then jump-cuts from being unkempt to blow-dried and straight. Throughout the entire video, the 1987 song "Never Gonna Give You Up" by pop singer Rick Astley can be heard playing in the background.

The video quickly went viral and started her YouTube career. According to an article in the *New York Times* by Amy O'Leary, the video quickly became popular and was viewed five million times during its first week. As of September 2018, the video had over sixty-seven million views.

After the success of "How to Trick People into Thinking You're Good Looking," Marbles continued to work at Barstool Sports.

For a time, Dave Portnoy featured the video on the Barstool Sports website. Six months later, Marbles decided to leave her job at Barstool Sports to pursue a career making YouTube videos.

Marbles eventually thanked Portnoy on her Twitter page for her job at Barstool Sports. On May 13, 2016, Marbles tweeted, "And thank you Dave for everything. We can make sure it's on my tombstone some day okay?"

Later the same day, Marbles also tweeted, "And that thank you is for @YouTube as well, thanks for making the coolest video machine ever. Love- one of your children."

CHAPTER THREE

The Queen of YouTube

B y the end of 2010, Jenna Marbles had only been posting videos for several months, yet she had already become very popular. On December 30, 2010, the brand and marketing magazine *Adweek* released a list of YouTube Trends on its website in an article by Megan O'Neill about the top ten most shared YouTube videos from that year. Marbles's video "How to Trick People into Thinking You're Good Looking" came in at number three.

According to the *Adweek* article, a YouTube personality named Keenan Cahill had created the number one most shared video of 2010. Cahill, who was fifteen at the time, suffers from a rare genetic disease that stunted his growth at the age of eight. In his video titled "Teenage Dream (Keenan Cahill)," Cahill lip-syncs to the then-popular song "Teenage Dream," by singer Katy Perry.

RAGS TO RICHES

While anyone can make a video and upload it to YouTube, it is very difficult to become popular like Jenna Marbles has. To

With often colorfully dyed hair, Jenna Marbles sometimes appears in public and poses around the world for various news and media outlets.

earn money on YouTube, a video will need to be popular, and the channel will also need to be monetized. A monetized YouTube channel has advertisements that can run before the videos. Each time someone watches an ad on YouTube, a small amount of money is earned for the owner of the channel. When a video like Marbles's "How to Trick People into Thinking You're Good Looking" becomes popular, it can earn a lot of money.

To help her decide what video might become popular, Marbles will often ask her fans through polls on her Facebook account. Marbles often gets many silly suggestions, such as eating soup with a fork, waxing a friend's armpit, or dressing up as Barry Manilow. Marbles's unconventional videos have made her very popular and wealthy.

According to a *New York Times* article by Amy O'Leary, "Ms. Mourey would not disclose any financial details, but industry experts estimate that a star at Jenna Marbles's level could make a very comfortable six figures from advertising revenues." The article also stated that "TubeMogul, a video ad-buying platform in California, examined traffic on the Jenna Marbles channel and estimated that she could have earned as much as $346,827.12 in 2012."

Soon after becoming popular on YouTube, Marbles decided to move to California. In Cambridge, Massachusetts, she had been paying $800 for a shared three-bedroom apartment. Thanks to her YouTube profits, Marbles was then able to move into a $1 million townhouse in Santa Monica, California, in 2011 with her boyfriend at the time, Max Weisz. Marbles and Weisz broke up at the end of 2012.

In 2013, while out with friends one night at a bar, Marbles met her current boyfriend, Julien Solomita. At the time, Solomita was working as a bartender when Marbles convinced him to take a night off and hang out. The two became friends first and soon began dating. As of 2019, they were still together.

On October 16, 2014, Marbles posted a YouTube video titled "House Tour Vlog," in which she explains how she moved again, to the San Fernando Valley, in Los Angeles, California. During the video, Marbles takes a tour of the large house with her dog Kermit while she narrates. In the video, Marbles says, "I don't own this place, just like I didn't own my last place."

Speculation in the media regarding Marbles's earnings continued. According to a 2015 *Forbes* article by Betsy Schiffman, "By most estimates, her

Jenna Marbles and her longtime boyfriend, Julien Solomita, met in 2013. The two have gone on to work together professionally on YouTube, radio, and a podcast.

START YOUR OWN YOUTUBE CHANNEL

Starting your own YouTube channel to share videos with friends and family can be fun and exciting. There are several things to consider before getting started.

- Get permission from your parents first.
- Create an account with Google, which owns YouTube.
- Be sure to use a unique user name and a strong password that has eight or more characters, with a mix of symbols and numbers.
- Use the instructions on YouTube's Create a New Channel page to get started.

To create videos for YouTube, you can use the camera on your mobile phone, tablet, or laptop. Remember to make your videos appropriate for everyone to see. It is a good idea to view recorded footage before uploading it. Many mobile devices have simple video editing apps that will allow you to cut unwanted footage. You can also use the YouTube Creator Studio page on a desktop computer to make simple edits to a video. Taking time and care to produce videos will help you create something that people may enjoy.

It's important to know that having a career on YouTube like Jenna Marbles is very difficult. To help people find your videos on YouTube, you can add hashtags. If you were uploading a video of a cat playing with a ball, you could use hashtags like #cats, #pets, #animals, and #funnypettricks.

[Marbles's] income is well into the six figures, and possibly as high as several million dollars."

MARBLES AND PROFANITY

Sometimes Jenna Marbles will use profanity in her videos. On the internet, anyone can become exposed to the use of profanity or obscene language, depending on what he or she is reading or watching. YouTube is no exception. According to a nonprofit group called Common Sense Media that rates websites for parents, Marbles is appropriate for children ages fifteen and up.

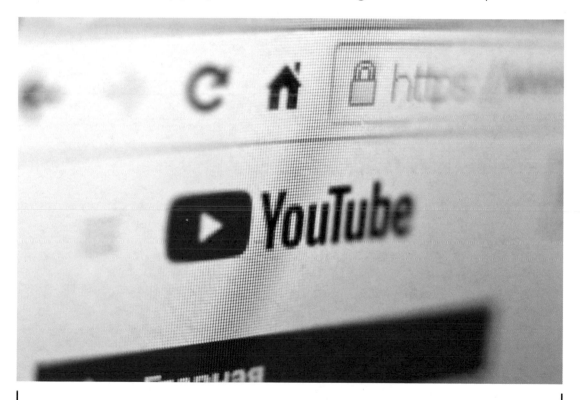

The video-sharing platform YouTube has become very popular with young people, who often watch gamers and online celebrities and upload and share their own content.

In 2016, YouTube updated its terms of service and took steps to limit the use of inappropriate content and language on channels that had been monetized. After the update, if YouTube determined that content or language was inappropriate, then that video could be demonetized and stripped of its advertising. This would make it impossible for content creators such as Jenna Marbles to make money from a video that contained profanity or content that YouTube deemed inappropriate.

On September 5, 2016, Jenna Marbles and her boyfriend, Julien Solomita, dedicated a full episode of their joint YouTube show, the *Jenna & Julien Podcast*, to speak out against demonetizing YouTube channels for the use of profanity. While none of her videos had been demonetized, she said, "The real issue is censorship. And that we use YouTube, as YouTubers, as a platform. We use it as a community. We use it as a place of discussion for a free and open exchange of thoughts and ideas, ah, where people can be themselves and talk about what they want, and say what they want … and reach a lot of people doing it."

CHAPTER FOUR

YouTube and Beyond

O n July 21, 2016, Jenna Marbles uploaded a video to her YouTube channel titled "Ultimate 100 Coats of Things Video." In the video (which is sped up quickly at times), Marbles applies one hundred coats of makeup, false eyelashes, and lipstick to her face. At one point, Marbles uses a hair dryer on her face to help dry the many layers of wet makeup. She laughs and jokes throughout the video as her face becomes more and more unrecognizable.

The makeup video ends with several close-ups of Marbles's face before she begins to wipe off the makeup. At the end of the video, Marbles says, "We're never doing this again. And we're never talking about it again either. When you go to bed tonight, just say like a prayer for my skin. I'd really appreciate it."

As of November 2018, the "Ultimate 100 Coats of Things Video" had been viewed more than sixteen million times, with 589,000 likes.

Marbles's popularity can be attributed to her many other unique, personal, and often wacky videos. While similar videos are at the core of Jenna Marbles's personal style and brand,

Jenna Marbles appeared at the Ghostbar Dayclub at the Palms Casino Resort in 2014 in Las Vegas, Nevada, where she met fans and signed autographs.

she has branched out, moving away from her YouTube channel as her sole media venue.

JENNA & JULIEN PODCAST

In 2013, Jenna Marbles and Julien Solomita began dating. Soon, Solomita began to appear on a few of Marbles's YouTube channel videos as well as her other, less frequently used YouTube vlog channel, JennaMarblesVlog. As time went on, they moved in together, and Solomita became a regular in Marbles's YouTube videos.

Solomita also has his own YouTube channel, TheFightingSolo, which had more than 1.6 million followers as of November 2018. The description on Solomita's YouTube page says, "I make videos documenting my life. I intensely enjoy creating an experience through my videos that draws from my own, while also playing with that dynamic and making it interesting for both of us. Often included are my girlfriend Jenna, and the furry kids; Peach, Kermit and Marbles."

On August 8, 2014, Marbles and Solomita hosted their first video podcast for their new YouTube channel, *Jenna & Julien Podcast*. A podcast is a digital audio file or music that can be downloaded over the internet onto a computer or mobile device for listening. Solomita had previous radio experience from his job at Amp Radio while he studied at Chapman University.

The introduction text below each *Jenna & Julien Podcast* episode says, "Welcome to the Jenna & Julien Podcast where we talk about all the things. If you are looking for your everyday, normal, by the book podcast, then you're in the wrong place. We created this because we tend to have awesome, random,

The streaming service Twitch has become a popular website to share, play, and watch others play video games. Twitch also has an app for mobile devices.

and sometimes drunk conversations that we realized had to be shared with the lovely internet world. So here we are."

As of February 2019, there had been 219 *Jenna & Julien Podcast* episodes, which can all be accessed on various platforms, including Spotify, Apple iTunes, and SoundCloud. Marbles and Solomita release a new podcast episode every Monday.

The couple also started a Twitch gaming stream together in 2016 where viewers can watch them play games.

SIRIUSXM SATELLITE RADIO

In July 2014, Marbles began hosting a weekly pop-music show on SiriusXM satellite radio. Marbles's show, *YouTube 15*, runs for one hour and airs every Friday at 6:00 p.m. Eastern Standard Time on Channel 2, SiriusXM Hits 1. The show was created in a deal between YouTube and SiriusXM.

According to an article by Todd Spangler in the June 26, 2014, issue of *Variety* magazine, Marbles said, "I'm incredibly excited to be working in a new medium with SiriusXM ... I think we are going to make a really cool show, and I'm honored that they picked me to do it."

During the weekly show, Marbles introduces new popular music as well as offers her comical commentary. In addition to listening live, *YouTube 15* is also available on SiriusXm on demand, and video playlists from the show are featured on SiriusXM's YouTube channel.

In 2018, the two created a website, Jenna Julien, where fans can find their podcasts, watch Twitch streams, and buy *Jenna & Julien* merchandise. The website also links to the couple's social network feeds such as Twitter and Instagram.

On May 16, 2018, Marbles released her four hundredth YouTube video, "We Bought a House." In the video, she and Solomita announce that they have just bought a house together. As with her previous moves, Marbles takes a short video tour of the spacious house for her audience.

SOCIAL MEDIA

In addition to YouTube, SiriusXM, and Twitch, Jenna Marbles can also be found on various social media sites. Marbles has verified public accounts on Twitter, Instagram, Facebook, and Snapchat.

Jenna Marbles's Facebook page, @jennamarbles, contains photos, videos, and information about her. There is also contact information posted for her fans who wish to email her, as well as a link to her YouTube page. In the Personal Information section, Marbles has a short bio posted. Just below it, Marbles says, "Thanks for being my super awesome friend on Facebook, I hope you found what you were looking for, and if you do, will you tell me what it is? Because I don't know what my life is about. Haha, thanks forever, Jenna."

WAX FIGURE: JENNA MARBLES

Madame Tussauds is a famous wax museum that started in London, England, over two hundred years ago. Today, Madame Tussauds has many locations in America, Asia, Australia, and Europe. The museum creates life-sized hand-sculpted wax figures of celebrities, film characters, sports stars, and historic figures. In the New York City location, visitors can see wax figures of famous people such as Jennifer Aniston, Johnny Depp, and President Donald J. Trump.

On July 23, 2015, Jenna Marbles announced on her Instagram page that she would be getting her likeness created in wax at the Madame Tussauds New York City location. According to her Instagram post, Marbles said, "I'm so beyond honored and excited that @nycwax is making me into a wax figure!! In October at their Times Square location you can come take selfies with wax me … this is probably the coolest thing that has ever happened I'm just so completely floored by this and thank you so much."

On October 26, 2015, Madame Tussauds unveiled the wax figure of Jenna Marbles. Marbles became the first wax figure of a social media celebrity created by the famous museum. At the unveiling, Marbles took selfie photos with her mobile phone while standing next to her wax likeness. Marbles also took photos of her boyfriend, Julien Solomita, as well as several friends and members of her family. She posted the pictures and a short video on several of her social media accounts.

Jenna Marbles poses with her wax figure likeness during its unveiling at Madame Tussaud's wax museum in New York City on October 26, 2015.

CHAPTER FIVE

Marbles Down the Road

As Jenna Marbles's popularity on YouTube increased, she began to make public appearances at events, at award shows, and on various forms of traditional entertainment, like film and television. She also started commercial endeavors, such as selling clothing on her joint website with Julien Solomita and creating a line of plush dog toys based on her own dogs, Kermit, Worm, and Mr. Marbles.

MARBLES IRL (IN REAL LIFE)

Many fans of Jenna Marbles may want to contact her IRL (in real life) or even find where they could meet her in person. Marbles has appeared at various public events and met some of her fans face-to-face. Fans who wish to contact Marbles can use various forms of social media like Twitter, Instagram, and YouTube to leave comments on her feed, or DM (direct message) Marbles. Marbles also has a contact email address listed on her Face-book page, contact@jmarbles.com. Anyone who wishes can use that publicly posted email address to write fan mail to Marbles.

Jenna Marbles signs an autograph while she poses with a fan during the annual VidCon festival and creator conference at the Anaheim Convention Center on June 24, 2016, in Anaheim, California.

Jenna Marbles has also appeared at these universities and international internet technology conferences:

- Web Summit is an international internet technology conference that began in Dublin, Ireland, in 2009. In 2017, Marbles spoke at Web Summit in Lisbon, Portugal. As of 2018, Web Summit had conferences in Asia, Europe, and North America.
- In 2018, Marbles spoke at another web conference, RISE, which was held in Hong Kong. During the RISE conference, Marbles talked about her large and loyal fan base and generating authentic content. According to an article

on the financial social network Gooruf written by Kingsley Man, Marbles said at the conference, "The numbers are in the back of your mind, but it's about being true and authentic, so it's important that our audience invests in us as people. Do something that fulfills you and your audience." On September 21, 2018, Jenna Marbles spoke to students at Slippery Rock University in Pennsylvania. Marbles was the first speaker of the academic year at the school. She spoke about her rise to fame and the importance of getting an education, and her fans—some of whom were in the audience—dressed up.

The 2017 technology conference Web Summit, held in the Altice Arena in Lisbon, Portugal, featured Jenna Marbles as one of many to speak about the influence of technology.

The Slippery Rock University newspaper, the *Rocket*, reported on the event on September 26, 2018. While onstage, Jenna spoke about her fans and said, "[My fans] are really, really cool and really awesome, and I get a lot of messages from people that are like, 'I was going through something really hard and difficult in my life and just watching you paint your face like a chair just made me forget about my life for a little while.'"

MARBLES MEDIA

It's very easy for anyone to see Jenna Marbles by going to her YouTube channel and watching any of her hundreds of archived videos. While there is a lot there, and binge watching it all would be a serious undertaking, there are other forms of media that Marbles has appeared in. According to IMDb, Marbles has fourteen acting credits, as well as having appeared as herself in over twenty TV shows. A few of the things Marbles has appeared in are:

- *Epic Rap Battles of History* is a short YouTube series that has different personalities face off against one another in a rap battle song format.
- Jenna Marbles appeared dressed up as Eve in season 2, episode 13 of *Epic Rap Battles of History* in the episode titled "Adam vs. Eve." Episodes of the show can be found on her YouTube channel, as well as the Epic Rap Battles website.
- *Ridiculousness* is an MTV show that collects and shows comedic viral videos and clips from the internet. As of August 2018, the show was in its eleventh season.
- Marbles appeared in an episode of *Ridiculousness* called "Jenna Marbles" in season 4, episode 10. The IMDb page

for the episode describes it, saying, "Internet sensation Jenna Marbles and Rob breakdown the web's best 'Face Lookers,' people whose injuries are 'Selfie Inflicted' and the recent 'Nerf-pocalypse.'"

- Smosh is a popular comedy channel on YouTube as well as a website. The Smosh website has videos, articles, and a store where a variety of Smosh-themed merchandise is for sale. In 2015, *Smosh: The Movie* was released. Jenna Marbles appeared in the PG-13 comedy film as herself.

MARBLES IN THE WILD

Chance encounters with Jenna Marbles in real life do happen. On December 6, 2018, Marbles and Solomita were in a mall in Los Angeles, California, shopping and videoing their trip as they went. They were creating a video called "Taking My Dog to Meet Santa," which they uploaded to YouTube that same day. In the video, Marbles and Solomita have Marbles's dog Kermit with them and are visiting the mall to take pictures with Santa. Afterward, a young boy named Joey (who was eating a cup of sprinkles) saw them in the mall filming, approached, and inquired if they had a blog channel and how many followers they had. Marbles laughed at the question, and Solomita jokingly replied, "Um, I don't know. A couple. I'm working on it though."

The boy then revealed on camera that he has his own YouTube channel, Joey Vlogz. He later excitedly returned to Marbles and Solomita after he finally recognized who they were. Joey Vlogz wound up in a Jenna Marbles video posted on December 6, 2017. Before Joey Vlogz appeared on Jenna Marbles's YouTube video, he had 185 subscribers. Soon after Marbles posted the video with Joey Vlogz, his YouTube channel shot up to a staggering ninety thousand subscribers!

WHAT NOT TO DO ... A FAN SHOWS UP

People who become famous sometimes have fans show up unannounced where they live. This is never a good idea. Fans should never bother celebrities, and they should only meet and engage with a celebrity at public events where they are expecting to meet people.

On September 17, 2017, Julien Solomita posted a video on his You-Tube page, TheFightingSolo, titled "Don't Come to Our House." In the video, Solomita explains how he and Marbles had recently returned from being away to find a stack of strange packages on their doorstep. He explained that while he was retrieving the packages, a mother and her son drove up and asked if Jenna Marbles lived there. Knowing that fans were looking for Marbles made Solomita feel unsafe and uncomfortable. In the video, Solomita told viewers not to come to their house and said, "Please don't do it. There are so many other ways you can connect with us that are appropriate."

Solomita concluded the video by asking fans to respect his and Marbles's privacy and not to engage in intrusive activities that make them feel unsafe.

Jenna Marbles meets fans at events like the 7th Annual Streamy Awards in Beverly Hills, California, held in 2017.

On December 8, 2017, only two days later, Joey Vlogz posted his own excited video called "It's A Holiday Miracle!!! (Thank You to Jenna and Julien)," thanking Marbles and Solomita for including him in their YouTube video. In his video, Joey Vlogz told his new larger audience how excited he was to have so many new followers so quickly as a result of the chance mall encounter. Way to go Joey Vlogz with a Z!

Fandom 250 is a website that ranks different fan bases for sports teams, entertainment, individual celebrities, and brands. In 2017, Jenna Marbles's fan base was voted number one in the Internet Famous category.

The Jenna Marbles fan base is loyal because Marbles continually presents herself as authentic. She is herself in her videos and does not hide her feelings and thoughts, even if they are unpleasant. Marbles's fans relate to her and her comical videos and upbeat personality.

TIMELINE

1986 Jenna Marbles is born on September 15.

2004 Marbles graduates from Brighton High School in Rochester, New York. Marbles moves to Boston to attend college
at Suffolk University.

2005 PayPal employees Jawed Karim, Steve Chen, and Chad
Hurley launch YouTube.

2008 Marbles graduates from Suffolk University with a degree
in psychology. Marbles begins graduate school at Boston University.

2010 Marbles graduates from Boston University with a master's
degree in sports psychology and counseling. Marbles
begins working for Barstool Sports. Marbles uploads her
first video on February 17, called "Charles Franklin Marbles Is a Sad Sad Man." Marbles uploads her first personal
video to her YouTube channel on July 9, called "How to
Trick People into Thinking You're Good Looking."

2013 Marbles begins dating Julien Solomita. Marbles is featured
in an April 12 *New York Times* article, "The Woman with 1
Billion Clicks, Jenna Marbles."

2014 Marbles begins hosting a weekly pop-music show on SiriusXM in July. Marbles and Solomita host their first video
podcast for their new YouTube channel, *Jenna & Julien
Podcast*, on August 8.

2015 Madame Tussauds unveils a wax figure of Jenna Marbles
on October 26.

2018 Marbles's YouTube channel hits more than eighteen million
subscribers in September.

GLOSSARY

blog A web page that is regularly updated with commentary or articles.

commentary Narration or an explanation about an event or situation.

DIY Do it yourself; the activity of making something yourself instead of buying it.

DM A direct message.

IRL In real life.

jump cut Quick editing cuts made in a video.

master's degree A higher-level college degree that can be pursued after earning a bachelor's degree.

monetization The ability to turn a service into an exchange of money.

podcast A digital audio file or music that can be downloaded over the internet onto a computer or mobile device.

pseudonym A fictitious name.

satirical Using humor, irony, or ridicule.

sports psychology A field of science dealing with the psychology of performance in sports or exercise.

streaming Transmitting data continuously over a computer network, especially live on the internet.

subscriber A person who signs up for a service.

tutorial A form of instruction in which a person models how to do something.

undergraduate The college years before earning a degree.

upload To transfer from a computer to the internet.

vlog A video log or online video posts.

YouTuber A person who frequently posts to the video website YouTube.

FOR MORE INFORMATION

Canada Safety Council

1020 Thomas Spratt Place
Ottawa, Ontario, Canada
   K1G5L5
(613) 739-1535
Website: https://
   canadasafetycouncil.org
Facebook: @canada.safety
Twitter: @CanadaSafetyCSC
The Canada Safety Council
   provides support and tips
   for staying safe online.

Extra Life

c/o Children's Miracle Network
   Hospitals
205 W. 700 South
Salt Lake City, UT 84101
Website: https://www.extra
   -life.org
Facebook, Twitter, and
Instagram: @ExtraLife4Kids
Extra Life uses online gaming
   to support users' local hos-
   pitals, raising money for sick
   and injured children.

Federal Trade Commission

600 Pennsylvania Avenue NW
Washington, DC 20580
Website: https://www
   .consumer.ftc.gov
Facebook:
   @federaltradecommission
Twitter: @FTC
Instagram:
   @federal trade-commission
The Federal Trade Commission
   has consumer information
   about online safety, privacy,
   identity, and security.

Junior Achievement

One Education Way
Colorado Springs, CO 80906
(719) 540-8000
Website: https://www
   .juniorachievement.org
Facebook and Instagram:
   @JuniorAchievementUSA
Twitter: @JA_USA
Junior Achievement is an organization that prepares young
   people to succeed in business and entrepreneurship
   efforts by providing programs in financial literacy
   and economics.

Media Smarts

205 Catherine Street, Suite 100
Ottawa, Ontario, Canada K2P
1C3
(800) 896-3342
Website: http://mediasmarts.ca
Facebook and Twitter:
@MediaSmarts
Media Smarts is a center for
digital and media literacy
that provides programs
and resources for homes,
schools, and communities
in Canada.

**YEC Young Entrepreneur
Council**

745 Atlantic Avenue
Boston, MA 02110
(484) 403-0736
Website: https://yec.co
Facebook: @yecorg
Instagram: @YEC
The Young Entrepreneur Council is an invitation-only
organization for young
people interested in starting their own business or
becoming entrepreneurs.
Find out if you qualify or
research the benefits of
the organization.

FOR FURTHER READING

Birley, Shane. *How to Be a Blogger and Vlogger in 10 Easy Lessons.* London, UK: Qed Publishing, 2016.

Cannell, Sean, and Benji Travis. *YouTube Secrets: The Ultimate Guide to Growing Your Following and Making Money as a Video Influencer.* Austin, TX: Lioncrest Publishing, 2018.

Ciampa, Rob, Theresa Moore, John Carucci, Stan Muller, and Adam Wescott. *YouTube Channels for Dummies.* Hoboken, NJ: John Wiley & Sons, 2015.

Downs, Alison. *Cool Careers Without College for People Who Love Fashion.* New York, NY: Rosen Publishing, 2017.

Furgang, Adam. *20 Great Career-Building Activities Using YouTube* (Social Media Career Building). New York, NY: Rosen Young Adult, 2017.

Giacboy97. *YouTube Planning Book for Kids Vol. II: A Notebook for Budding YouTubers.* Milton Keynes, UK: Beans and Joy Publishing, 2017.

Goold, Aaron. *The Video Editing Handbook.* Seattle, WA: Amazon Digital Services, 2017.

Stockman, Steve. *How to Shoot Video That Doesn't Suck.* New York, NY: Workman Publishing, 2011.

Tashjian, Janet. *My Life as a YouTuber.* New York, NY: Henry Holt, 2018.

Willoughby, Nick. *Making YouTube Videos: Star in Your Own Video!* Hoboken, NJ: John Wiley & Sons, 2015.

BIBLIOGRAPHY

Fabian, Tom. "Jenna Marbles Speaks with Students About Life After College." *Rocket*, September 26, 2018. https://www .theonlinerocket.com/campus-life/2018/09/26/jenna-marbles -speaks-with-students-about-life-after-college.

IMDb. "Jenna Marbles." Retrieved October 5, 2018. https://www .imdb.com/title/tt3502124/?ref_=ttep_ep10.

Jenna Julien. "Podcast #1—Technology, Kids, and Useful vs. Useless Classes in School." Video. YouTube, August 8, 2014. https://www.youtube.com/watch?v=aYtXr7kBAIw.

Jenna Julien. "Podcast #107—The Censorship/Demonetization of YouTube." Video. YouTube, September 5, 2016. https:// www.youtube.com/watch?v=dZK8N_tk2is.

Jenna Julien. "Podcast #139—Julien Sucks at Celebrity Trivia: Music Edition 2." Video. YouTube, May 1, 2017. https://www .youtube.com/watch?v=T89Vt_NfxR0.

Joey Vlogz. "IT'S A HOLIDAY MIRACLE!!! (Thank You to Jenna and Julien)." Video. YouTube, December 8, 2017. https://www .youtube.com/watch?v=5oUfe5b-vTs.

Keenan Cahill. "Teenage Dream (Keenan Cahill)." Video. YouTube, August 28, 2010. https://www.youtube .com/watch?v=lm_n3hg-Gbg&index=2&list =PLDED153A52050B795&t=0s.

Man, Kingsley. "RISE Conference 2018: The Best Quotes and Key Takeaways (Day 3)." Gooruf, July 13, 2018. https://gooruf .com/asia/news/2018/07/13/rise-conference-2018-the-best -quotes-and-key-takeaways-day-3.

Marbles, Jenna. JennaMarbles. "Draw My Life—Jenna Marbles." Video. YouTube, March 28, 2013. https://www.youtube.com /watch?v=sCxzaHC30Ec.

Marbles, Jenna. JennaMarbles. "House Tour Vlog." Video. You-
    Tube, October 16, 2014. https://www.youtube.com
    /watch?v=S2x1T2D9J9s.
Marbles, Jenna. JennaMarbles. "How to Trick People into Think-
    ing You're Good Looking." Video. YouTube, July 9, 2010.
    https://www.youtube.com/watch?v=OYpwAtnywTk.
Marbles, Jenna (@jennamarbles). "I'm so beyond honored and
    excited that @nycwax is making me into a wax figure!! In
    October at their Times Square location you can come take
    selfies with wax me and grope da butt all you want. The grope
    zoo will officially be open jk but seriously this is probably the
    coolest thing that has ever happened I'm just so completely
    floored by this and thank you so much @nycwax." Instagram
    photo, July 23, 2015. https://www.instagram.com/p
    /5fCIZEp3u7.
Marbles, Jenna. JennaMarbles. "Taking My Dog to Meet Santa."
    Video. YouTube, December 6, 2017. https://www.youtube
    .com/watch?v=wp2rHoZ3GN8.
Marbles, Jenna. JennaMarbles. "The Mom Tag—Meet My Mom."
    Video. YouTube, November 26, 2014. https://www.youtube
    .com/watch?v=1WPhpiTnHjY.
Marbles, Jenna. JennaMarbles. "Ultimate 100 Coats of Things
    Video." Video. YouTube, July 21, 2016. https://www.youtube
    .com/watch?v=hsFLMjlgR_o.
Marbles, Jenna. JennaMarbles. "We Bought a House." Video. You-
    Tube, May 16, 2018. https://www.youtube.com
    /watch?v=-kTWIm7m4Uw.
Marbles, Jenna. "And that thank you is for @YouTube as well,
    thanks for making the coolest video machine ever. Love- one
    of your children." Twitter, May 13, 2016, 8:18 p.m. https://
    twitter.com/Jenna_Marbles/status/731277588182622208.
Marbles, Jenna. "And thank you Dave for everything. We can
    make sure it's on my tombstone some day okay?" Twitter, May,

13, 2016, 9:02 p.m. https://twitter.com/jenna_marbles
/status/731288437953728512.

Mulshine, Molly. "Why One of YouTube's Biggest Stars Refuses to Cash In on Sponsored Videos." Business Insider, August 13, 2015. https://www.businessinsider.com/jenna-marbles -explains-her-youtube-business-model-2015-8.

O'Leary, Amy. "The Woman with 1 Billion Clicks, Jenna Marbles." *New York Times*, April 12, 2013. https://archive.nytimes.com /www.nytimes.com/2013/04/14/fashion/jenna-marbles.html.

O'Neill, Megan. "Top 10 Most Shared YouTube Videos of 2010." *Adweek*, December 30, 2010. https://www.adweek.com /digital/most-shared-youtube-videos-2010.

Schiffman, Betsy. "Lifestyles of the Rich and YouTube-Famous." *Forbes*, October 14, 2015. https://www.forbes.com/sites /betsyschiffman/2015/10/14/youtube-jordan-maron /#5f26d4d143b3.

Solomita, Julien. "Description." YouTube. Retrieved October 5, 2018. https://www.youtube.com/user/TheFightingSolo /about.

Solomita, Julien. "Don't Come to Our House." Video. YouTube, September 17, 2017. https://www.youtube.com/watch ?v=3HcoFZv6_AE.

Spangler, Todd. "YouTube Pacts with SiriusXM for Weekly Music Radio Show with Jenna Marbles." *Variety*, June 26, 2014. https://variety.com/2014/digital/news/youtube-pacts -with-siriusxm-for-weekly-music-radio-show-with-jenna -marbles-1201251012.

Spangler, Todd. "YouTube Star Jenna Marbles: 5 Facts About Her Rise to Internet Fame." *Variety*, July 18, 2013. https:// variety.com/2013/digital/news/youtube-star-jenna -marbles-5-facts-about-her-rise-to-internet-fame -1200564607.

INDEX

ABOUT THE AUTHOR

Since he was a teenager, Adam Furgang has created countless home-brewed videos and has had his own YouTube channel since 2013. He attended the University of the Arts and has worked as a graphic designer, web designer, fine artist, photographer, and finally … a writer. His current writing credits include numerous nonfiction books in the middle school market. He is the author of *20 Great Career-Building Activities Using YouTube*, in the Rosen Social Career Building series. He lives in upstate New York with his favorite photo subjects—his wife, two sons, and his dog, Gizmo Jones.

PHOTO CREDITS

Cover, p. 1 Michael Tullberg/Getty Images; pp. 5, 21 Monica Schipper/Getty Images; p. 8 Paul Brady Photography/Shutterstock .com; p. 9 Michael Bezjian/WireImage/Getty Images; p. 13 Africa Studio/Shutterstock.com; p. 14 © AP Images; p. 15 Stephanie Diani/The New York Times/Redux Pictures; p. 20 Don Arnold/ WireImage/Getty Images; p. 23 sub job/Shutterstock.com; p. 26 Mindy Small/FilmMagic/Getty Images; p. 28 Allmy/Shutterstock .com; p. 31 Cindy Ord/Getty Images; p. 33 FilmMagic/Getty Images; p. 34 Horacio Villalobos/Corbis News/Getty Images; p. 37 David Livingston/Getty Images; additional interior pages design elements krystiannawrocki/E+/Getty Images (blue light pattern), Yaorusheng/Moment/Getty Images (yellow background).

Design and Layout: Michael Moy; Editor: Xina M. Uhl; Photo Researcher: Nicole DiMella